THIS BOOK
BELONGS TO

_____

_____

A LITTLE OWL BOOK
FUNNY FEET

by Clive Hopwood

illustrated by Stewart Liptrot

WORLD

In the world there are lots of feet,
Some are big, some small and neat,
Some look strange, and some look strong,
Let's see to whom they all belong!

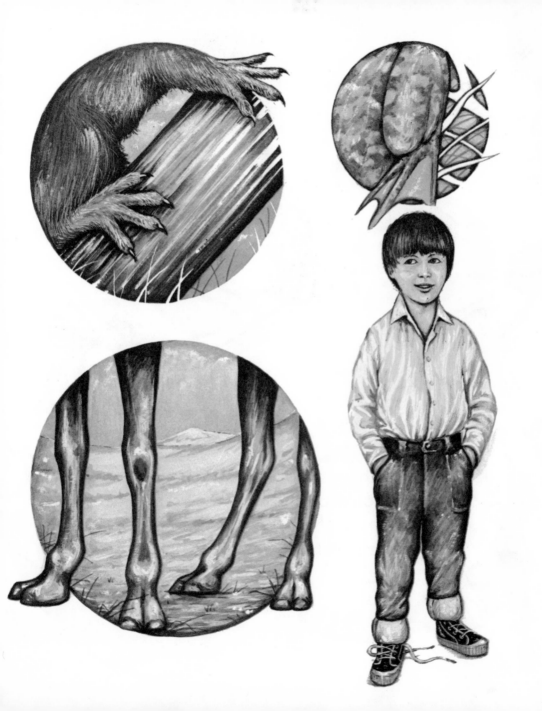

With whiskers trim and soft, warm fur,
If you stroke her now she'll purr .
In front of the fire – that's where she's sat,
These feet are paws, they belong to a . . .

CAT

Squeaking, scampering, how fast they go,
They keep well clear of cats, you know;
They live in fields, or in a house,
Have you guessed that these are the feet of a . . .

MOUSE

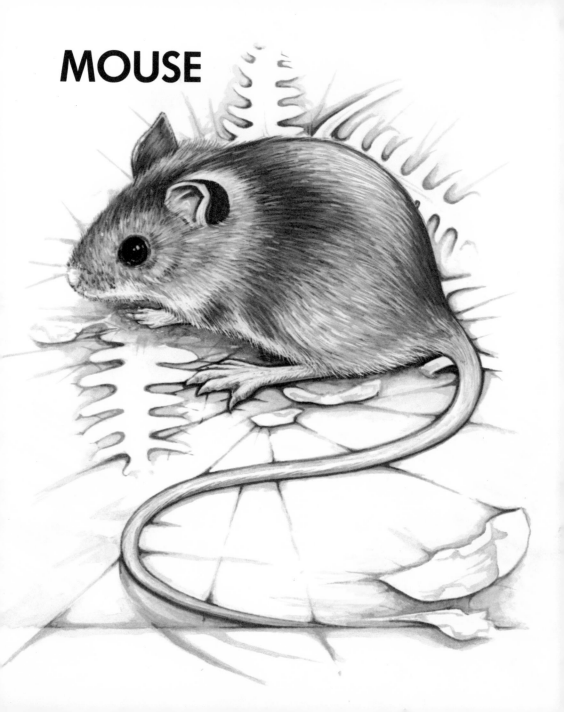

Working hard the whole day long,
Its buzzing sounds just like a song,
Making honey for our tea,
These six little feet belong to a . . .

BEE

Galloping, cantering, along his way,
Give him some sugar, give him some hay;
This one you'll guess, it's easy of course,
His feet are called hooves – they belong to a . . .

HORSE

If you go down to the farm you'll meet
These swimming birds with bright, webbed feet,
Quacking and splashing – with any luck
You'll know these feet are those of a . . .

DUCK

The babies live in a pouch on their Mum,
And they leap and bound when they want to run;
Its feet are large, its tail is too,
Yes, these feet belong to a . . .

KANGAROO

Off to the zoo for a treat today
We see some creatures there at play;
How funny they look, having their tea,
These are the feet of a . . .

CHIMPANZEE

Long trunk, large ears, and great big feet,
What do you think he likes to eat?
What he likes best is a tasty plant,
A jungle beast, the . . .

ELEPHANT

Hunting for fish, he uses his paws,
Breaking the ice with big, sharp claws,
Huge and white, all covered in hair,
Yes, of course, it's a . . .

POLAR BEAR

What strange creature have we here?
Don't worry, it's not one to fear!
Just turn the page and then you'll see,
It's someone just like . . .

We walk, we run upon our feet,
So keep them warm and dry and neat;
Without them we could never stand –
Just you try walking on your hands!